Liking Myself

By Pat Palmer, Ed. D.

like me

Illustrated &
Handlettered By Betty L Shondeck

This book is dedicated to my children,

Penny and Betsy,

and to the child in each of us.

Copyright © 1977, by Pat Palmer

Twelfth Printing, August, 1989

LIBRARY OF CONGRESS CATALOGING IN PUBLICATION DATA

PALMER, PAT, 1928–
  LIKING MYSELF.

  SUMMARY: AN INTRODUCTION TO CONCEPTS OF FEELINGS, SELF-
ESTEEM, AND ASSERTIVENESS.
  1. SELF-ACCEPTANCE – JUVENILE LITERATURE. 2. EMOTIONS –
JUVENILE LITERATURE. 3. INTERPERSONAL RELATIONS – JUVENILE
LITERATURE. (1. SELF-ACCEPTANCE. 2. EMOTIONS. 3. INTERPERSONAL
RELATIONS) I. SHONDECK, BETTY L. II. TITLE.
BF697.P26   158'.1   77-88185
ISBN: 0-915166-41-0

Impact 🐚 *Publishers*

POST OFFICE BOX 1094
SAN LUIS OBISPO, CALIFORNIA 93406

Table of Contents

To the Young Reader

This book is yours for fun. It is full of ideas, exercises and questions for you.

It is full of warm thoughts and love.

Ask your parents to read it with you.

Enjoy this book.
Enjoy yourself.
Enjoy being You!

Liking Yourself

Part 1

It is OK
to like yourself
and be
your own good
friend.

When you need a friend,
do something nice for yourself like:

Play with a kitten...

Walk a dog...

Sing...

Bake cookies

Draw a picture...

... Whistle...

Play the piano...

..... Dance...

Climb a tree...

.. Smile...

Write down or draw your _favorite_ things to do.

Do one nice thing each day as a
special gift to yourself.

Being a good friend to yourself means that:
...you can [STOP] doing something you don't like,

...you don't have to like everybody,
...everybody doesn't have to like you,

...you can rest when you are tired.

Doing what :you: want to do is important!

Being a good friend to yourself means...

...you can say nice things to yourself.

What a nice smile!

Write down or draw some nice things you can think or say about yourself.

Also, being a good friend to yourself means...
that it is OK to think about the things
you can do.

Write down or draw some of the things you can do.
(Don't worry if you're not "super-good." Nobody's Perfect!)

When you hear yourself saying mean things
to yourself say, "STOP"!

Replace the mean thought with one of the
nice things about you.

I can jump high!

I can bounce a ball!

I can jump rope!

Say to yourself, "I am lovable and valuable," every time you walk through a door...

enter a car...

I am lovable and valuable!

PET SHOP

come to a stop sign...

STOP

Do this for two weeks,

...and...

you will <u>feel</u> lovable and valuable!

Get some exercise every day to keep your body happy.

running

jumping

swimming

Playing tag

bicycling

baseball

hiking

skating

Write down or draw the kinds of exercises _you_ like to do.

Keeping your body happy helps to keep the rest of you happy.

Liking yourself and being your own good friend helps you to like other people and be a good friend to them.

It is fun to give other people a treat, such as...

...scratching their backs...
(the way you like it, too!)

You bake GOOD Cookies!

...sharing your favorite cookie...

...telling them nice things you like about them.

...giving them turns on your bike...

Share the good parts of you with others!

Enjoy being <u>you</u> right now!

Clap your hands...

Give yourself a hug...

Smile at yourself...

Be happy to be <u>you</u>!

... Now ...

Take some time

to go over what you have learned
about

♥ liking yourself ♥

before you go on to the next part of the book.

Part 2

Feelings

Feelings are good friends.

Feelings let us know...
what is happening,
what we want,
what is important to us.

glad
happy
feeling good
ok
so-so
unhappy
sad
mad

Feelings are like a thermometer.

Pay attention to your feelings inside of you.
They tell you that you are...

lonely

cold

hungry

sad

angry

scared

glad

happy

Listen to your feelings. They tell you when you
need to take care of yourself, like finding a friend
if you feel lonely, crying if you feel sad, singing
and smiling if you feel happy, and acting frisky
if you feel good.

We can pretend not to feel, but we still have feelings anyway. Below are some strong feelings that everyone has once in awhile. Put a check (✓) by the ones you have felt.

— I feel _lonesome_.

— I _love_ baby animals.

— I feel _sad_.

— I am all alone and _scared_.

— I feel silly.

— I _like_ to swing

— I _like_ my best friend.

— Sometimes I feel _helpless_.

— When I am _tired_ I feel _down_.

— Sometimes I get _mad_ at mother.

— Circuses are _exciting_!

— Playing ball is _fun_.

If someone you love is hurt, leaves, or dies, being
full of pain and grief is OK.
Boys and girls, ...
   men and women... .
      all have feelings ...
all need to be able to cry once in awhile.

It is OK to show your feelings!

Let yourself feel even the hard feelings, because...
holding them back 🤚 and ✋ them 🔽 inside just
pushing   down

makes them stay . . . .
                and stay . . . .
                        and stay . . . .
              and keep hurting.
Let out the hurt feelings as fast as you can!
You don't need to hold on to them.
Let go of them so that they can leave.

Many men believe that to be manly, a man shouldn't show any feelings, so a big strong man isn't supposed to cry, to feel hurt, to be scared, to need help, or to feel lonesome. Trying to be a big strong man is like trying to be King Kong. You have to pretend not to be <u>human</u>! You have to not let people see the <u>real</u> you. If you pretend not to have feelings long enough, one day you may not feel anything any more, or at least you may not know what feelings you are feeling!

Can you figure out what you are feeling
<u>right now</u>?

It is better to be sad and cry, if you feel
that way, than to   hold it in and try
<u>not</u> to feel it.

... And... it is better to be happy and laugh,
if you feel that way,
to share it with others.

A lot of people like to pretend that some feelings aren't there.

A favorite one to pretend away is anger.

- Write down or draw some other feelings that people don't like to talk about.

... Anger is an OK feeling...

It tells you when someone is stomping on your flowers.

It tells you neat things about yourself, like ...

...how you want to be treated ...

....what you think is fair...

...things that you think are important...

• Write down or draw some of the things <u>your</u> anger helps you to know about yourself.

It is OK to be angry when someone stomps on your flowers!

Anger that is saved, and saved, and saved,

may explode into violence,

may cause you to be sick,

i have a tummy ache again

may lead you to hurt others,

either with words,

or with fists.

Inside...

Your feelings help you to know what is right for <u>you</u>.

Feelings help you to decide what...

...to do
...to say
...to try
...to like
...to not like.

Feelings <u>are</u> good friends!

··· Now ···

Take some time to go over what you have learned about

Feelings

before you go on to the next part of the book.

32

Feeling Talk

Part 3

Feeling talk is saying what you
feel or think
without hurting or upsetting others.

Talking about feelings hurts no one.
If I say, "I am angry,"
that doesn't hurt you.
If I say, "I am lonely,"
that lets you know me better.
The secret is to start by saying,
"I think," "I feel," "I want."

I Think, I Feel, I Want Game

1. Ask a friend to be your partner.

2. Sit facing your friend.

3. Talk with your friend, starting each sentence with either "I think," "I feel," or "I want."

4. Share with your partner how it feels to talk starting each sentence with "I."

5. What happened? Did you learn anything new about your partner? Did you discover anything new about yourself? What kinds of things did you learn?

Another secret to good feeling talk is <u>not</u> to say to another person, •"<u>You</u> are...(dumb, stupid, mean)," •"<u>YOU</u> did it...," or •"<u>YOU</u> make me mad."

When you are mad, talk about how <u>you feel</u> and maybe why you feel that way, but <u>not</u> about other people.

Calling others names makes <u>them</u> feel bad, or upset, or mad at you. What happens to <u>you</u> when someone calls you a name? How do you feel when someone gets mad at you?

Feeling words are good friends...
They help you to tell what is going on inside of you.
Here are some feeling words. Can you think of some more?

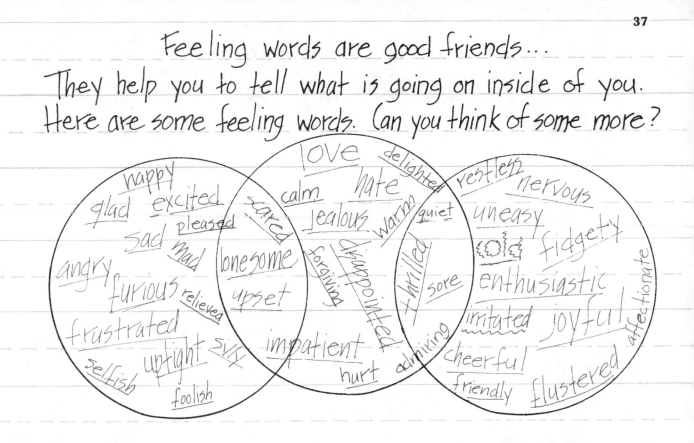

Feeling Talk Game

1. Ask a friend to play with you.
2. Stand facing each other.
3. Use feeling talk to act out (pretend) a time when:
    - One of you asks to borrow something and the other says "No."
    - One of you has just stepped on the other's toe.
    - One of you has just broken the other's bike.
    - One of you forgot to return a pencil.
    - One of you has just lost a favorite pet. It was hit by a car.

4. Add more real life times in which you would like to practice using Feeling Talk.

When you talk about a feeling no one has to do anything or say anything, unless they <u>want</u> to.

...So, if your friend is late and you say, "I'm really upset. I've been waiting for 20 minutes for you and I'm mad." You feel better. Your friend knows that you are upset about being late. But you didn't call your friend "stupid" for being late.

When you talk about your feelings, no one needs to feel guilty, bad or punished. You are just talking about how <u>you</u> feel, and what has happened to <u>you</u>.

Sometimes it feels scary to say your feelings to adults. It can help to practice feeling talk with people who are in charge. Practice with a friend. Pretend your friend is your mother, father, teacher, principal or another adult. Tell the pretend adult....

- How you feel about him or her.
- How you feel about something very important to you such as a sadness, something that hurts you that the adult does or says, a feeling of deep love, or a problem with a friend.
- That you think a rule is unfair or won't work.
- About a real life situation that is bothering you.

Remember to use feeling talk!

Sharing and Caring Game

1. Ask a friend or family member to be your partner.

2. Sit facing each other.

3. Take turns telling each other the things you like about <u>each other</u>.

4. Take turns telling each other the things you like about <u>yourself</u>.

5. Be sure to listen to each other.

Everyone needs love.

Feeling talk is a way of talking about...

...loving

I love you!

I like your smile!

...feeling sad

...giving compliments

I feel sad today

...liking

...being angry

I'm really upset. I have been waiting...

... sharing and caring ...

NOW

Take some time
to go over what you have learned about

Feeling Talk

before you go on to the next part of the book.

Allowing

Part 4

You can be different from everyone else, and still be OK

Allow yourself to be human.
Humans have feelings.
Humans are warm and loving.
Sometimes even humans like to...

...climb trees...

slither through the jungle...

roar roar like a lion...

baaaa like a sheep...

...or even mess things up...

weep like a weeping willow...

...jump like a kangaroo...

Being human is nice!

Allow yourself to be you...

to be...

rare...

beautiful...

individual...

1 of a kind award

unusual

...opposite

...different

special...

·Write down or draw some of the things about _you_ that are ¦special¦

It is OK to be different!

The Difference Game

1. Sit down with your friend.
2. Tell the things about you that are different from your friend.
3. Ask your friend to tell you the things that are different from you.
4. Ask your friend the things he or she likes about you.
5. Tell what you like about your friend.

I really like your hair.

Allow yourself to make mistakes. Sometimes you may feel badly for making a mistake,... like forgetting to come home on time, or pulling out the bottom can in a supermarket and causing a crash, or forgetting to do something you were supposed to do.

<u>But</u>... the most important thing is to fix your mistakes! Help stack up the cans again! Be home on time today!

Allow yourself to think of mistakes as a way of learning how to do things better. Then, making a mistake can be OK. Also, remember that it is not fair to others or to yourself to use, "I made a mistake," as an <u>excuse</u> for being careless, or for not doing your job, or for hurting others.

• List a few mistakes that taught you something.

. . . Did you fix them?

Allow yourself to change your mind ...

You can become a doctor instead of a nurse ...

You can change your favorite color...

You can change your favorite game ...

...or movie

or food ...

... or story...

You can decide to like yourself...
   instead of not liking yourself.

You can change your <u>mind</u>... or...
   <u>yourself</u>
                        anytime.

• Write down or draw <u>one</u>
change <u>you</u> would like to
work on.

Allow yourself to do things "just because."

You don't have to have a reason for everything.

You don't have to explain everything you do.

Having a "why" for everything isn't necessary.

Doing what you want to do is OK...

as long as ...

you don't hurt anyone...

or make them feel bad.

Allow yourself to be you. You don't have to pretend to be someone else ...or act like someone else... or copy someone else...or talk like someone else...or look like someone else.

You can relax and just be you!

Allowing yourself to be happy causes happy things to happen to you. Nice thoughts color your life happy colors. Being nice to yourself, being your own good friend, helps others to be nice to you, too, and to be your friend.

•Draw a picture of yourself with happy colors.

Being good and kind to yourself helps all
the people around you like <u>themselves</u> and <u>you</u>!

•Draw your own smile and wear it!

Now...

Take some (time) to go over

what you have learned about...

Allowing

before going on to the next part of the book.

Body Talk

Part 5

Your body
talks
to you
all the time.
Learn how to listen!

Check your body right now.

· Do you take deep ⬇ breaths?

· Do you slouch in your chair?

· Is your lower back tight?

· Is your stomach tight?

· Are your knees locked?

· Is your fist clenched?

· Is your jaw tight?

· Is your neck relaxed?

· Do you have a headache?

· Are your shoulders up high?

· Do you chew your fingers?

Take a few very deep breaths and

let go

of the tightness in your body.

Your body wears out faster when it is held tight.
Your body gets sick if it is held tight all the time.

Learn to listen to your body; check it out often,
and
let go

when it feels tight.

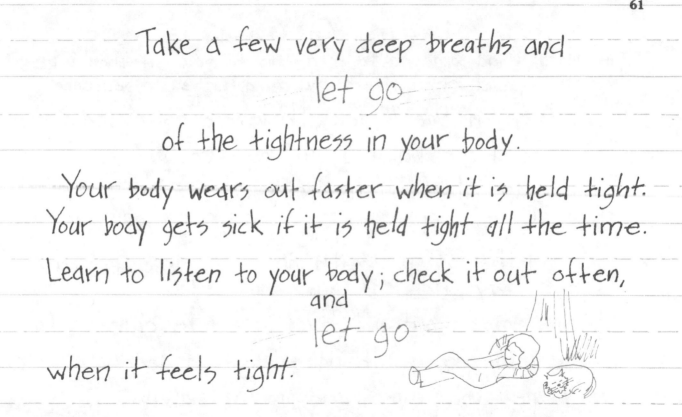

Letting Go Game

Directions: Find someone to read this to you. It should be
read slowly with pauses after each sentence.

·Lie down on the floor with your eyes closed.

·Feel the floor holding up your body.

·Take a deep breath all the way down to your tummy.

·Slowly let it out.

·Take another deep breath and this time fill up
your body and legs with air.

·Slowly empty out all the air. ·Lie quietly for
a few minutes, breathing slowly and deeply.

·Open your eyes, and sit up slowly.

Sunshine Game

Lie on the floor or a bed with your eyes closed. Be aware of your breathing. Take some deep breaths down into your belly. Let your body become very heavy.

Imagine a tiny speck of light in your belly. Slowly let it expand. Very slowly it will fill your belly with light, energy and warmth. Gradually the light spreads throughout your body. It is like sunshine. You are filled with energy.

Very slowly take the light into your body. When you are rested and filled with energy, open your eyes. Sit up when you are ready.

Keep in touch with your body feelings.

If you pay attention to body messages,
    you'll know when things are OK...
        ... are wrong...
        ...are the way you want them.

You can use your body energy...
    to change things if you need to ... or
    to enjoy things when they're OK.

Now

Take some time
to go over
what you have learned
about

Body   Talk

before you go on to the next part of the book.

66

Part 6

Letting Go

Some things get better when you
let go...

...like...
δ loose tooth...

...δ hot pan...

Ouch!

When you love a puppy, mouse, or kitten,
you let it go to be and to act like itself.
•Draw a picture of your favorite pet or one you would like to have.

It is good to learn to let go when you love someone.

So... you learn to let friends go...
to be ...
and
to do...
what is important to them.

By allowing and letting go
of friends and loved ones,
you free them
to be themselves.

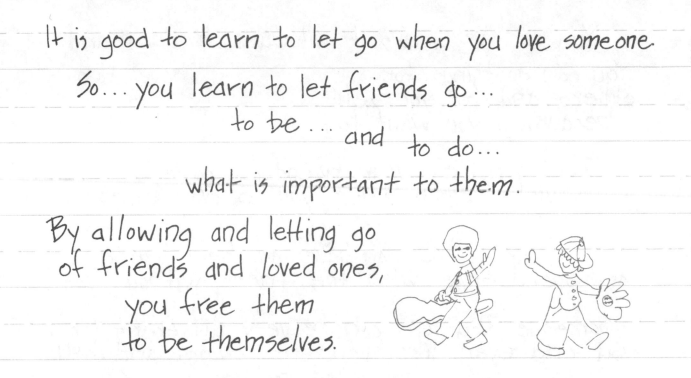

You can be yourself without "shoulds" and...
You can do things for   "have to's."
others and for yourself...
...because ... you want to!

For instance... your friend can go to a
   violin lesson while you go play baseball.

      Your friend can have another friend...
and spend time with this friend without you.

Someone you love can be very different from
you and even like different things and still
            be loved by you.

When your body is tight, letting go of the tightness feels good.

When your head hurts, you can relax and let go of the pain.

When you are afraid, saying it out loud helps to let it go.

When you are angry, saying, "I'm angry!" lets the anger out and helps it to go away.

Let go of the idea that everyone
has to like you.

• Does the baker have
to like you to sell
you a cake?

• Does the doctor
have to like you to
treat your measles?

• Write down or draw some people you can work with who
don't have to like you.

Let go of the idea that
      if someone doesn't like you,
   you are bad... or you have failed.

Let go of the idea that in order to be liked
you _have_ to do what someone else wants you
to do. If you spend all your time doing
what others want you to do ...

You never get a chance to be yourself!

A pretzel person meets everyone's needs, tries to be liked by everyone, and does anything others want.

A pretzel person has no opinions, no special likes or dislikes, and stretches to fit into whatever is happening.

A pretzel person lets other people make decisions, like choosing the movie, the kind of birthday cake, the game to play, where to go and what to do.

Are you a pretzel person?
If so... let go!

STOP being a pretzel person.
· by being who you are,
· by making decisions,
· by having opinions,
· by having likes and dislikes,
· by saying what you want and don't want.
It is OK to be you!

Let go of the idea that what you want
will come to you if you <u>wait</u>.

No one can read your mind.
<u>Ask</u> for what you want.

People who love you ... don't know ...
what you're thinking.

Let them know.

Wishing is OK, ... but asking is faster.

Wanting is OK, and asking will get you what
you want more often...

like a hug... or... a birthday party

Let go of the idea that you can't ask for what
you want. (But don't expect to always get it).

- Write down or draw some of the things you would like to ask for.

Let go of the idea that men and boys have to be strong and can't cry, or can't show feelings, such as ... fear or ...love or ... tenderness.

And...

let go of the idea that women and girls have to be weak and always cry and have softer feelings, and can't take care of themselves.

Men, women, boys and girls are _all_ _human_.

We all have feelings.

We all can be... strong, or weak, or afraid or angry.

It is nice to be able to cry,
  · or feel sad,
    · or say you are scared,

· or that you hurt,

        or that you care.

i'm scared!

i care about you!

And it is nice to be strong
            and to help others.

It is nice to be human!

You can find your own strength and power.
You can learn what feels best to you.
You can let go and allow yourself to be,
and... you can

Like Yourself

and be your own good friend,

and

a good friend to others, too!